# TAKE-OUT

## Sonnets about Fortune Cookies

# TAKE-OUT

## SONNETS ABOUT FORTUNE COOKIES

BY

## KIM BRIDGFORD
DAVID ROBERT BOOKS

Published by David Robert Books
P.O. Box 541106
Cincinnati, OH 45254-1106

ISBN: 9781936370085
LCCN: 2010936112

Typeset in Garamond
Cover Photograph: Jo Yarrington
Author Photograph: courtesy of the author

Poetry Editor: Kevin Walzer
Business Editor: Lori Jareo

Visit us on the web at www.davidrobertbooks.com.

# ACKNOWLEDGMENTS

I am grateful to colleagues and students who contributed fortunes to this project: Iris Bork-Goldfield, Kay Cosgrove, Elizabeth Ferris, Brian Harniman, Cathy Miners, Zach Miners, Susan Rakowitz, and Jo Yarrington.

I am especially indebted to Cathy Miners who has done a statistical analysis of the lucky numbers—with unexpected results.

I appreciate all of the efforts Kevin Walzer and Lori Jareo have made in the service of poetry, as well as their longstanding support of my work.

Finally, I thank my son Nick for opening bags of fortune cookies with me, helping me find the most interesting fortunes, and coming up with the title for my book; and my husband Pete, whose fortune and mine have been the same since 1987.

***

*The American Poetry Journal:* "The Elephant in the Room"
*The Barefoot Muse:* "Gossip"
*First Things:* "Stringed Instrument"
*The Listening Eye:* "Originality"
*The Long Islander:* "The Ship"
*Measure:* "Generosity and Perfection," "Surprise Party"
*New Zoo Poetry Review:* "Good Manners"
*Poem:* "Of Course"
*Seems:* "Change," "Discontent"

For Pete and Nick

# CONTENTS

# I.

*Learn Chinese—Pot Sticker*
*Guo-tie*

# SURPRISE PARTY

*Don't let unexpected situations throw you.*
*Lucky Numbers 33, 14, 27, 16, 37, 49*

Instead embrace the shock of people leaping
Out from behind your furniture and drapes:
Forget you felt your years were slowly creeping,
Fossilizing into yours for keeps.

Laugh at the mugs proclaiming hills you're over,
The black balloons, the silly underwear,
Victoria's Secret, strings not made for cover,
The wine lined up for years you cannot bear.

And if you hate surprises, would have liked
A solitary dinner, know that others
Will have that fear of numbers, just like you.
It's best to grab some punch (of course, it's spiked),
Then put your birthday arms around what bothers,
And tell the breathless crowd, "I never knew."

# STRINGED INSTRUMENT

*Don't spend time stringing and tuning your*
*instrument. Start making music now.*
*Lucky Numbers 33, 2, 37, 48, 1, 26*

So what if your strings break. How many strings
Does someone need? Make smaller music then,
And if your instrument is out of tune,
Do not despair. Play melancholy songs.

This fetishizing takes a lot of time—
The strings intact and sounding as they should,
The concert-goers waiting for what's good.
(The same is true when worrying a rhyme.)

Just play. And if it's not quite what you thought,
Remember that, so often, errors heard—
The ones that woke you up, caught in your throat—
The audience missed. Don't reach for what is hard.
Convince yourself that there is no lost ground
Between perfection and what's merely sound.

# THE SHIP

*Don't wait for your ship to come in; swim out to it.*
*Lucky Numbers 5, 17, 11, 34, 7, 42*

It is invigorating just to swim—
Activity that swerves from the pedantic.
Yet what if as you're paddling limb by limb,
The ship you're swimming to is the Titanic?

Perhaps that's just the way that poets learn,
That when they finally see the dream's true price—
The beauty of its shape from prow to stern—
It runs into a startling piece of ice.

Maybe it's better to keep it down to size,
The dream of glory destined to capsize:
Instead the ship that's making its last run,
Retirees on the edge of what was fun,
Or something smaller yet, for one or two,
The barely glimpsed tight smile of a canoe.

# THE ELEPHANT IN THE ROOM

*Don't kiss an elephant on the lips today.*
*Lucky Numbers 21, 4, 38, 49, 5, 11*

Choose another way to conduct yourself.
Don't kiss an elephant on the lips today,
As much as you might like to. Just play golf,
Or take a trip to feed your urge to play.

Don't kiss an elephant on the lips today.
If it's romance you want, check personal ads—
Or take a trip to feed your urge to play.
Don't be a prisoner to these passing fads.

If it's romance you want, check personal ads
(You might find elephants turn others on).
Don't be a prisoner to these passing fads,
But go for broke—the trunk, the lips, the skin,

As much as you might like to—or just play golf.
Choose another way to conduct yourself.

# GOSSIP

We like to think the world's in love with love,
But actually it's more in love with talk.
We like to think the world's view is above,
But it is not—nor does it walk the walk

Of those who suffer, or go against all odds.
No. It's the heat of public enterprise
That fuels the traveling talk to fantasize:
*He left his wife? How many hotel beds?*

Tongues now begin to click, and ears to listen
For someone else who knows the body's heat:
For love is not just sex but moral lesson,
Depending on who's happy and who's not,
Depending on what is and isn't said,
Depending on who's watching up ahead.

# THE MISTAKE

*When you make a mistake, do not treat yourself as*
*if though you were the mistake.*
*Lucky Numbers 5, 34, 11, 47, 8, 29*

There're coming at you, dizzy flocks of crows;
You try to shield yourself and your good name.
But they keep coming back. Each flutter knows
The entrails lying heated with your shame.

*It's a mistake*, you want to say, but you
See what you've done as irretrievable.
Their beaks are prying at your flesh like glue.
To stew in your own juices is a hell.

If you can only say you're sorry and move on,
But worthlessness is difficult to shed.
You find the crows are cawing in your head.
Their voices, low and raw, make you not listen

Until determination starts to cry,
*I will do better next time*, and they fly.

# II.

*Learn Chinese—Delicious*
*Hao-chi*

# CHANGE

*Change has both physical and psychological attributes.*
*Lucky Numbers 1, 24, 37, 5, 11, 48*

In wearing vintage clothes, Change shows he's hip;
His Levi 501s give time the slip
With bowling shirts that read both "Bud" and "Lou."
You never know what he is going to do.

And just when you predict it, there he is,
Adrape with velvet clothes that reek showbiz,
And vowels that must elongate for his mood,
The versatility of attitude.

There's something to the glitter of surprise
That pleases both the heart and startled eyes.
For most of us transform by increments
Like the unfurling secrets of our plants.
Change is motion with nostalgic sass,
The blur of what is written as we pass.

# BEYOND THE FINE PRINT

*After readying the every emotion, I see some*
*understanding peer entering realm.*
*Lucky Numbers 34, 11, 5, 18, 26, 4*

This is a fortune for the middle-aged,
Who hope the moving clouds of text will clear,
The words debated, print that's feather-edged.
What is that "the"? What part of speech is "peer"?

Translation's always difficult, the ways
To meaning fraught with many obstacles,
Just like this strain and struggle of the eyes.

This morning, gathering books out of my car,
I heard a colleague walking down the halls,
Reciting a poem, half like a song, and half
Like a prayer, the way we speak inside the self.

This floating artful praise is what we are.

This taught me to be patient, and to watch
The way a text will flare and start to catch.

# GENEROSITY AND PERFECTION

*Generosity and perfection are your everlasting*
*goals.*
*Lucky Numbers 5, 21, 30, 31, 32, 33*

I like that these two words are offered up
Together in a silver loving cup,
Two words we often don't think of together.
We're used to separating out our weather

And also words. And these two here, not yin
And yang, not like a salt and pepper shaker,
But more that one is reaching for the Maker,
The other handing out what once was in.

Although they both wear shining suits, does one
Have more to do with earth and one with sun?
Does one like thinking more of the abstract,
While the other puts its hands on literal fact?

Or is it simply where we end or start:
The clouds of heaven or the human heart?

# THE LEADERS

*A leader is powerful to the degree he
empowers others.
Lucky Numbers 24, 37, 15, 42, 38, 8*

This poem is for the women who were told
They didn't work, and raised their children well;
For ministers who know just how the old
Are breathless with the stories they must tell.

It's for the people who clean toilets so
Their children can have energy to dream;
It's for the teachers who sort false from true
And, through a piece of chalk, make knowledge gleam.

This is for nameless poets, friends, and those
Who after hurricanes sent food and clothes;
Who kept us safe, who ran to put out fires,
Created public space, exposed the liars.
This is for those who used each piece and scrap;
This poem is for most people on the map.

# SHELF LIFE

*Your ideals are well within your reach.*
*Lucky Numbers 47, 8, 39, 41, 25, 30*

Like jam or honey sitting on the shelf,
With labels you have printed out yourself,
Ideals are ready to be opened up,
And tasted on your bread or in your cup.

Like something that is stirred or thick on knives,
Ideals are ready for ordinary lives.
Sometimes we tell ourselves we must be noble,
But then ideals sit, unused, on the table.

Better they be put to common use,
Like tablecloths, wine glasses, or our joy.
Don't push them, like a vase or breakfast tray,
Into a spider's transitory lace.
One day, in seeing them, you'll hesitate
And realize the expiration date.

# WISDOM

*Every day is a new life to a wise man.*
*Lucky Numbers 20, 33, 47, 29, 5, 16*

Instead of seeing life as suffering—
Each day a weight that you are now enduring—
Be open to the day: not *carpe diem*
Exactly, but as if you're in a dream,

A place in which, like bowls of undrawn pears,
The incidents all take you unawares,
And in their curving shapes and tawny tones
Fall in a breathless way along your bones.

Remember that these pears are not just fruit
But the experience that comes from your pursuit:
And wisdom comes with light as drawings ripen,
And wonder lines the hand as moments deepen.
Refuse the daily dying of the soul,
And touch anticipation in the bowl.

# III.

*Learn Chinese—How much*
*Duo-shao qian*

# DISCONTENT

*Discontent is the first necessity of progress.*
*Lucky Numbers 18, 24, 37, 19, 8, 42*

I suppose it's what made Emily move up
Into her attic room—*Enough's enough*—
And feel the quiet like heaven, but a sip,
The place where she could contemplate what-if.

And yet both Sylvia and her friend Anne
Could not use discontent to make a plan,
Or could, approaching it much differently,
Where Death sat, meter on, inside a taxi.

For each of them, the discontent's removal,
Where life, for women, is based on men's approval.
They had to make a different kind of space
For books sewn up with thread, or Death's kind face.
I wonder, then, if discontent's a way
To realize the price you have to pay.

# SUPPORTING ROLE

*Do not worry about holding a high position*
*rather about playing your proper role.*
*Lucky Numbers 5, 14, 28, 7, 42, 36*

Polonius, I understand your role,
As many women do, behind the screen.
You have a lot in common with the queen,
Who knows how passion takes what passion will,

And uses it. And then there is Ophelia,
Whose death is just support for the idea
That Hamlet must compel himself to act,
If he can sift the fiction free from fact.

So much must happen that we do not say
Except behind the curtains, and off-stage.
I know some women who will fold their rage
In the creases of embroidered handkerchiefs,
And no one is the wiser. O brief play
That's written in the margins of our sleeves!

# SENTIMENTALITY

*Don't accept that others know better than
you.*
*Lucky Numbers 22, 17, 49, 5, 33, 10*

You've found that men can be most sentimental
About their wars, their past, their westward-ho—
The vast expanses of their buffalo—
Their jobs, their poses snapped before the mantel;

Their baseball games; experience with sex;
Their children; college bouts with alcohol;
Their relationships with Mother—all complex—
Their legacies; their friends; their kiss and tell.

And yet when women start to write their poems,
To write their lives, relationships, and homes,
They are described as trivial, sentimental,
Focusing on what is largely ornamental.
It's not the feeling then: just grand or small,
And who says which is which, which makes it all.

# THE HAMMER AND THE ANVIL

*It is better to be the hammer than the anvil.*
*Lucky Numbers 6, 23, 18, 44, 28, 19*

It is better to have power than to not;
It is better to be strong than to be weak.
It is better to show action than show thought.
It is better to deliver blows than ache.

It is better to be wind that sweeps the hill
Than be the children who are vulnerable.
It is better to be showing off one's strength
Than showing mercy by the yard and length.

While some say this, I much prefer the view
Of the hammer and the anvil to renew
What's broken, and through creativity
Reshape what's seen as a dichotomy.
How little difference between "and" and "than";
How different in significance for man.

# ORIGINALITY

*Originality overcomes everything.*
*Lucky Numbers 5, 28, 19, 37, 7, 4*


I must admit this puts my mind at rest.
I thought convention, with fascistic zest,
Stamped with its boots the different, weird, and strange,
The new idea dancing on the fringe.

I'm glad that fear is out and bold is in.
I'm glad we want to push the envelope.
I'm glad to hear that *Huckleberry Finn*
Won't make a city wash its mouth with soap.

No longer do we have to question why
There's art, or why an astronaut should try
To walk the starry beaches of the sky.
It's good to hear that what's creative will
Win out through ingenuity and skill.
It hasn't happened yet, and yet it will.

# COTTON CANDY, BRIDES, AND PEYTON MANNING

Homecoming queens, watch out, and apple pie,
TV evangelists, and candy bars,
The models who sell beer, and sex, and cars,
The country singers who tell their girls good-bye.

Red wine with bread and cheese, beware, and flowers
Arriving in a scented paper cone.
O lottery and all the sunset hours
Along the beach, your loveliness has gone.

This sticky, overwhelming love, like flies,
Has come to me by fortune's TV voice,
And redirects what's fickle, unencumbered.
Consider now the emcee's glittering eyes,
The audience *oohing* at the lights and noise,
Forgetting, for a time, its days are numbered.

# COCKY

*Over self-confidence is equal to being blind.*
*Lucky Numbers 12, 13, 14, 19, 20, 39*

This metaphor that shows a lack of sight
Underscores that you do not live right.
And whether you showboat, or think your poem
Is the equivalent of ancient Rome,

Your way of parenting the only way,
Your car the one that caps the B on eBay,
You need to take a pause. Enough's enough.
Sometimes it isn't good to strut your stuff.

Sometimes what you don't see is that the rest
Will turn away, or roll their eyes. You're lost,
And the drum roll that you feel is admiration
Is really nothing but the consternation

That what you see is no one else but you,
And this negates the rest of what you do.

# A KNOCK ON THE DOOR

*Don't worry; prosperity will knock on your door soon.*

*Lucky Numbers 9, 27, 15, 34, 4, 22*

And he's brought wine, a deep and lovely red,
And you will offer him some crusty bread,
And you will speak at length into the night,
While finishing your meal by candlelight.

And he will say that what you say is true:
Your vision now has found the right milieu,
That now you will experience happiness,
Where recently was heartache, worry, loss.

Prosperity makes easy what was hard,
Like friendship that is offered by the yard.
And when he leaves, how late the moonlit hour,
How much you know you'll miss what's now a blur
Of happiness, and wine, and a belief in you.
By morning you'll believe it isn't true.

# IV.

*Learn Chinese—School*
*Xue-xiao*

# GOOD MANNERS

*Don't behave with cold manners.*
*Lucky Numbers 4, 12, 24, 30, 40, 44*

Your manners must not happen edged with ice.
They must not be just form without the spirit.
It's like pretending that you do not hear it
When someone calls your name, not once, but twice.

Your manners must live other than the snow.
They must not be the surface of the lake,
Or pines that whistle through their needles, "Go."
They must cause hospitality, not heartache.

Your manners must not burrow underground,
To sleep until a better time can surface.
You must make others feel the interlace
Of heart and fingers, while they shyly stand.

You must make others feel that they are known
When they are cold, and icy, and alone.

# A SLIGHT HESITATION

*Think before sharing with others.*
*Lucky Numbers 34, 28, 37, 18, 1, 38*

This fortune, opposite of courtesy,
May conjure pictures of a miser's gold,
The trickling nuggets where a soul is sold,
The archetypal warning against money.

Or else the glutton, tearing swinely flesh
And washing it all down with swigs of wine.
Or else the evil stepparent whose wish
Is that the children die in slow decline.

Yet what if time is what is substituted?
We should think how we would prefer to spend it,
Not squander what we have. We can't rescind it.
Our attitude is what's evaluated.
We should be sharing, as we seize the day,
Not be nostalgic as we walk away.

# THE TRAIL

*Do not follow where the path may lead. Go
where there is no path . . . and leave a
trail.*
*Lucky Numbers 12, 20, 37, 44, 36, 9*

We tend to think of life as two extremes:
The well-worn path or else the Amazon,
The one clichéd with other people's dreams,
The other huge, impenetrable, and green.

But how about the path that zags and zigs,
Unknown to you, and yet you're not afraid?
Occasionally a person in the twigs
Calls out, like thatchwork crafted out of shade.

Throw out your lonely tasting medicine
And look around. Sometimes you'll find a song,
And dusk, like heaven's multicolored thought,
Will fall. On other nights, it's interaction—
What people share with you of right and wrong—
That tells you what you are and what you're not.

# R.S.V.P.

*You may attend a party where strange*
*customs prevail.*
*Lucky Numbers 33, 12, 38, 44, 5, 49*

Everyone is naked, and you're not,
Or else the situation in reverse.
You can't depend on what your mama taught,
And drinking only makes conditions worse.

What's being eaten? Is that bird or rat?
Why are the people beating you with that?
Is that a dance or suicidal throng?
What fork is right, and which belief is wrong?

Such places have a dreamlike quality,
Because there are rules even when you party.
If you don't know them, you can't eat or sit,
Without a second thought to question it.

You hope you have a friend whose fortune is,
*Guide others through their opportunities.*

# I DON'T WANT TO

*Each day, compel yourself to do something*
*you would rather not do.*
*Lucky Numbers 36, 17, 2, 40, 33, 4*

Departmental minutes, you are mine,
And long lines stretching in the D.M.V.
Used car sales people, I ask you to apply,
And telemarketers, tie up my line.

I'm locked out of my house, and can't get in;
I've lost my passport, and cannot find my way.
My computer has just crashed; all poems, good-bye,
Which I must reconstruct from '91.

At parties, I am told I don't look well,
And I can't figure out the food I'm eating.
My airplane touches down in the wrong city.
Some look at me with both concern and pity,
What do I hear? The unofficial greeting
Of Kafka, who says, "Welcome. This is hell."

# TO KEEP IN MIND THAT

*You will find yourself in a position of*
*dignity in the end.*
*Lucky Numbers 23, 14, 27, 44, 5, 17*

But in the meantime, life will hit you hard.
You'll suffer, and the crowd will laugh at you.
They'll spread a rumor, and it won't be true.
Some days you'll find life shallow and absurd.

You'll want the world to see your worthiness,
Not just the times you faltered through duress.
You'll want the world to see your inner self,
Not just a statue, chipped and on the shelf.

Yet at the end you'll have a moment where,
As you curl up your skin and languish there,
You'll understand the paradox of life,
Your dignity a subtle leitmotif.
What's broken down and lonely is at peace.
Or is it just that shifting gears will cease?

# NO MISUNDERSTANDING

*Better to understand little than to*
*misunderstand a lot.*
*Lucky Numbers 7, 2, 41, 5, 18,*
*44*

I'd like to understand a little space of ground,
A grave, or garden, through my hands and flowers.
I'd like some smallness to while away my hours,
No vast horizons, dusted high by wind;
No spin of watered-down geography,
But rather what I know, a loss, a leaf.

A tending is a quiet side of grief.
I want the texture: gritty, shovel groan
And all the delicacy of shattered bone.

A lot sometimes protests the question "why?"
A little doesn't try to act, but is.

Touch the dirt, daily and mysterious;
Kneel and understand though bits of flint
And dirt, the knowledge of bewilderment.

# BEFORE YOU GO

*It may be well to consult others before taking*
*unusual actions.*
*Lucky Numbers 23, 14, 47, 8, 39, 5*

Before you pack your bag, and board your plane
To some far-off and dusty place, where stones
Are furniture and trees are broken bones,
And everything is measured by the sun;

Before you quit your job; desert the faith;
Take all the money waiting in the bank;
Before you die another daytime oath;
Before you stay up late, with one more drink,

Remember all the stories of the ones
Who walked into the world, did not return.
Like some strange logic of a lost and found,
Your life will fill with spices, voices, signs
That are used up like paper left to burn,
And you made weightless, like the least of sound.

# V.

*Learn Chinese—Good*
*Hao*

# GOOD SAMARITANS, APPLY

*We have too many sounding words and*
*too few actions that correspond with*
*them.*
*Lucky Numbers 13, 28, 7, 34, 11, 20*

If words are trumpet like, our deeds are not.
Or not enough. Who leaps to wield the sword?
Who sees the fox in pain, and untraps it?

So often with the elderly we're bored,
To hear, another time, a list of pain.
It's hard to hear *that* trumpet call again.

Perhaps that's what the problem really is.
We want the hyperbolic word and deed,
So that we fail at what cannot succeed.

Meanwhile the little dramas make us squirm.
They're not enough to dream upon for us.
So when we say good-bye it's falsely warm.

Outside the sky is blue with light cloud cover.
We're glad today's ordeal is finally over.

# HONESTY POLICY

*The truth is always bearable when told with
compassion.*
*Lucky Numbers 20, 14, 5, 28, 47, 30*

I don't think this is true, and here is why.
Most people love the shimmer of illusion,
The *what-if* even if there's not one try,
And we are fellow actors in collusion.

*We could have been; we almost were.* These words
Are what our dailiness is fed upon.
This is the appetizer served with wine
And what a sense of worthlessness affords.

A student told me that his father said
That life's the journey to find just how small
We are inside the scheme of nothingness,
That children think of vastness, not of dread,
Believing they're unique and beautiful.

Meanwhile, we like the sparkles on the dress.

# THE BURDENS

*Every burden is a blessing.*
*Lucky Numbers 6, 27, 46,*
*17, 8, 30*

This paradox is hard to understand.
Consider Job, or someone's relative,
Who suddenly has lost the will to live.
What is deserved gets lost in desert sand.

Because, of course, we think that we are owed,
With all our goodness treasure in our sack.
We want just what we've earned: not this cold ache,
Not dying friends, or love's delinquent mood.

But agony is not mathematical,
And once we free ourselves from this, it's better.
We do not make our fortunes by the letter,
Or suffer through the rules grammatical.
We are the stubborn, solitary tree
That learns through wind to grow more crookedly.

# BELIEVER

*Your heart is pure, and your mind clear, and*
*your soul devout.*
*Lucky Numbers 26, 34, 17, 26, 39, 30*

I picture people clothed in black or white,
Their lips aflame with Biblical caress,
The soul stripped back to what it is at night,
The naked lit by murmured holiness.

And this is what I think when I'm afraid,
My self that's offered to a hurricane
Or death, to see if I might make a trade.
I pull the world away and see divine.

It is this moment like a circle lit
Before the blue and hallowed shape of Mary
Or the many-thorned surrender of her son
That makes us see that we are only one
Among the many who are sad and who are sorry
For who we are. Belief's our amulet.

# THE PASSWORD

*Courtesy is the password to safety.*
*Lucky Numbers 5, 18, 26, 37, 29, 24*

I think of lips that whisper hidden signs
To circumnavigate the world's designs,
The underground that runs with breathless steps
To crevices beneath commuter maps.

The eyes that peer out, almost in the dark,
While Gestapo boots search out their human mark.
The family huddles, folded in like bats,
While thinking of both Shakespeare and the rats.

And while our daily lives are not intense—
Or filled with danger and the wind's suspense—
I find that courtesy does take us to a place
More delicate that we can interlace
With shapes and sounds that we do not yet know.
The gentleness with which I speak will make it so.

# VI.

*Learn Chinese—Bean Sprout*
*Dou-ya*

# RISK

*Accept the next proposition you hear.*
*Lucky Numbers 34, 19, 27, 3, 17, 5*


How easy it would be to just say *yes:*
To one more drink, resort land for a song,
With worries not about what might go wrong,
But all the tax evasions you'd finesse.

A quick romance? A happy Vegas marriage?
Why not? Who doesn't want the Elvis glitter
Surrounding a romance that's sure to matter
At least until next week, with lucky steerage?

It's easy to say *yes.* Just try again,
The way you would the notes along a scale.
*No*, as an answer, always lacks a heart.
When Anna Karenina died beneath a train,
And Satan fell from heaven with his court.
You felt the shame, but whispered, *Beautiful.*

# SETTING GOALS

*Keep your goals away from the trolls.*
*Lucky Numbers 44, 5, 26, 8, 38, 9*

We think that time and laziness and age
Will strip us of our dreams and of our goals,
But now we find they're vulnerable to trolls.
Perhaps it's time to pause, to set the stage

For what we see ourselves as living for.
If fairy tales can seize what we're about,
Then maybe what we're in should be what's out.
Or maybe this is just a metaphor

For all the magic, out from under bridges,
That we walk past because we are too old.
In such a subtle way our dreams are sold.
We have to pull our goals out from the edges,

And whether it's a troll or time or breath,
We have to take a risk or risk our death.

# THE GOAL

*A goal is a dream with a deadline.*
*Lucky Numbers 45, 23, 16, 2, 46, 26*

There is a point at which a dream has weight,
And you find that you no longer hesitate
To work for what you want: your distant star
Gets closer. You have traveled to the future.

And much the way someone in films will fly
To distant galaxies, where tendrils open
And the flowers swoon with what they know will happen,
So too is there inevitability

In what you've made an hour at a time.
You are now someone other than you seem.
You're someone who has lived to see the dream.
While some give up when picturing the climb,

There are others who set out, and breathe what's good:
It's a matter of both height and attitude.

# JUST TUNE IN

*Wow! A secret message from your teeth!*
*Lucky numbers 2, 34, 17, 22, 38, 40*

This makes me think of teeth that pick up noise,
The breathless innuendo of small boys,
Detective work that through a cavity
Unveils the underworld's depravity.

How strange to think of what can come through teeth,
The secret codes imbedded in the mouth,
And like a radio that picks up song,
Your dental work picks up a world gone wrong.

I'd love to be in such communiqué
That ordinary life would fall away—
A James Bond sitting in the dentist's chair,
Perfecting narratives out of the air.
Perhaps that's where imagination lies,
The ordinary taken by surprise.

# TRANSFORMATION

*Your secret desire to completely change your life will*
       *manifest.*
*Lucky Numbers 23, 17, 28, 33, 15, 40*

Routines you have will all be stripped away,
And there you'll be, cut loose from history.
Your cardboard figure will be lit by fame,
With glitter at the edges of your name.

You picture living on some vague white beach,
With turquoise water, a hut made out of thatch;
And yet you've never liked your loneliness.
Better to stay home, with all its stress.

Better just to want hyperbole.
You want just what you have, with swelling music
(A god in a machine might do the trick).
You want the van to drive up. There you'll be,
Crying that you can't believe it's you,
While everything inside you says you do.

# OF COURSE

*There's no such thing as an ordinary*
*cat.*
*Lucky Numbers 20, 34, 12, 7, 38, 2*

There's no real way to disagree with that.
A cat will place its faith upon the air,
Believing in the solid of somewhere.
There's no such thing as an ordinary cat.

There's no real way to disagree with that.
It brings a mouse as gift, or else a bird,
The way a poet springs upon a word.
There's no such thing as an ordinary cat.

There's no real way to disagree with that.
A cat and poet place themselves outside,
And find an open place in which to hide.
There's no such thing as an ordinary cat.

A dog's superior? Don't tell me that.
If you want beauty, there's the poet-cat.

# CAT AND MOUSE

*When the mouse looks upon the cat, there must*
*be an escape route nearby.*
*Lucky Numbers 22, 34, 48, 2, 47, 5*

This cat and mouse philosophy is true
When we take off much more than we can chew.
Sometimes we need to have a back-up plan,
However much we take life with élan.

It's better if we follow both the mice
And friends who have the following advice.
Wait for the door that's open, and slip through.
Wait for the bits of birdseed as your cue.

Learn to take the slip, and squeeze through gaps.
You'll have the run of houses in collapse.
You'll have the freedom larger creatures don't.
They say that they will catch you, but they won't.

When someone hears you running, you can trick
Foundations into settling into music.

# THE SEED

*Every adversity carries with it the seed
of an equal or greater benefit.
Lucky Numbers 9, 15, 17, 28, 6, 41*

At first, we turn our backs on this small seed,
And wonder how we'll take another breath.
It's hard to find the goodness in a death.
We stand in lines of black, and sob our need.

Where is the place that opens up to us—
The heaven-stairs to the miraculous—
And makes us happy in our waves of gloom?
Where in our seedlessness is room

For one that brings us happiness to measure
To match our loss, equal or greater treasure?
The dirt we rub between our fingers will
Be indiscriminate in what to pull

A life from: worm, a bit of tree, a flower.
We have to be as open to life's power.

# AFTERWORD AND BIOGRAPHIES

Running the lucky numbers of this project through statistical analysis proved interesting and surprising. The attached statistical charts prove that the lucky numbers in the fortune cookies are not random, but humanly generated *to look like* random numbers. The typical lucky numbers are under fifty, not consecutive, and the numbers people are likely to bet on: birthdays, ages of children, etc.

The next time you check your lucky numbers, remember that it's like looking in a mirror (not a cookie!). The lucky numbers reflect the numbers you want to see and the chance nature you like to think of in a cookie, all crafted by a human being.

# LUCKY NUMBERS ANALYSIS

Table A: A comparison of the 113 sets of lucky numbers from the fortunes in the sonnet sample and 113 sets of six numbers between 1 and 50 selected using Excel's random number generator.

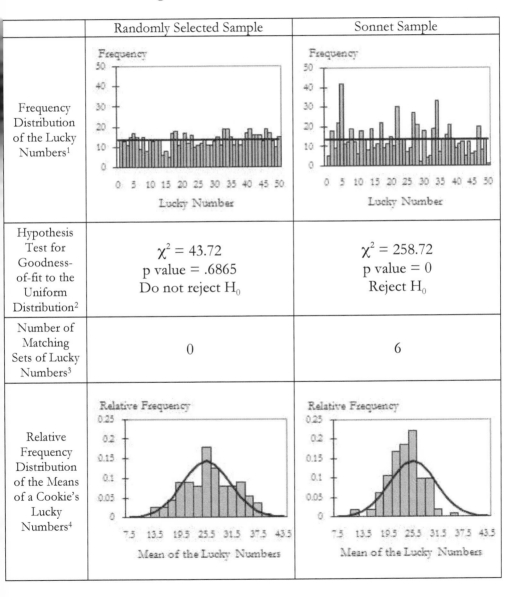

| | Randomly Selected Sample | Sonnet Sample |
|---|---|---|
| Frequency Distribution of the Lucky Numbers[1] | | |
| Hypothesis Test for Goodness-of-fit to the Uniform Distribution[2] | $\chi^2 = 43.72$<br>p value = .6865<br>Do not reject $H_0$ | $\chi^2 = 258.72$<br>p value = 0<br>Reject $H_0$ |
| Number of Matching Sets of Lucky Numbers[3] | 0 | 6 |
| Relative Frequency Distribution of the Means of a Cookie's Lucky Numbers[4] | | |

[1] Given that the lucky numbers are randomly selected, the expected number of occurrences of a particular number is $(6*113)/50 = 13.56$. The horizontal line on the frequency distribution graphs marks this value.

[2] There is dependence within a set of randomly drawn lucky numbers because the lucky numbers on a particular fortune do not repeat (are drawn without replacement). The appropriate test statistic is Pearson's goodness-of-fit test statistic multiplied by the correction factor $(N - 1)/(N - k)$, where N is the number of numbers being drawn from and k is the number of selections. See Boland and Pawitan (1999). In this case, the correction factor is $49/44$. If the number of draws is sufficiently large, the statistic has a $\chi^2_{49}$ distribution. If each of the fifty possible lucky numbers is equally likely to appear on a fortune, the population of lucky numbers follows a uniform distribution. For the sonnet sample, the hypothesis that the population of lucky numbers follows a uniform distribution is rejected.

[3] Given that the six lucky numbers are randomly selected (without replacement) from the numbers 1, 2, ..., 50, there are 15,890,700 possible number combinations. With 113 draws, the probability of (at least) one match is .0004. For the probability of a match to be .50 (for there to be even odds of a match), about 4,694 draws are required.

[4] If n numbers are randomly selected from 1,2, ..., N, the mean of the selections is approximately normally distributed with a mean of $(N + 1)/2$ and a standard deviation of $((N + 1)(N - k)/12k)^{1/2}$. See Boland and Pawitan (1999). In this case, if the selected lucky numbers are truly random, the mean lucky number on a fortune is approximately normal with a mean of 25.5 and standard deviation 5.58. This normal curve is superimposed on the relative frequency distribution of the mean. Note that the frequency distribution for the randomly drawn lucky numbers is approximately symmetric while the frequency distribution for the sonnet sample is skewed left—there are more means below the modal class than above the modal class. This is characteristic of human-selected numbers. Individuals tend to over-select from the low end of the number pool because they rely on birth months (1-12), dates within months (1-31), number of children, etc. for their number selections.

Graph A: The relative frequency distribution of the minimum gap for the randomly selected and sonnet samples[1]

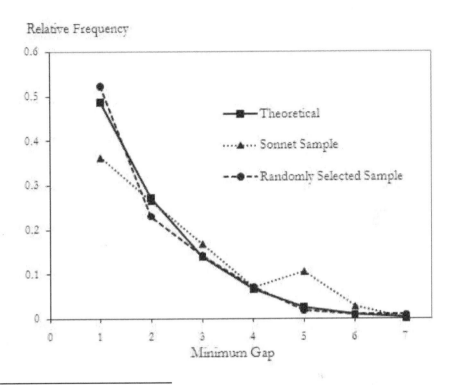

---

[1] The minimum gap is the smallest difference between the lucky numbers on a fortune.

The theoretical relative frequency distribution consists of the relative frequencies that are expected if a cookie's lucky numbers are randomly selected.

Note that the relative frequencies for the randomly selected sample track the theoretical frequencies, whereas the sonnet sample lucky numbers have fewer minimum gaps of 1 and more minimum gaps of 5 than expected if the selections are truly random. Compared to truly random selections, the lucky numbers printed on the fortunes in the sonnet sample are more spread out and less likely to contain consecutive numbers (numbers with a minimum gap of 1). This result is consistent with the strings of numbers generated by statistics students who were asked to create a set of random numbers from their heads. See Boland and Pawitan (1999). Even though a set of six randomly selected numbers between 1 and 50 has about even odds of consecutive numbers, it is the perception that consecutive numbers are unlikely.

The analysis suggests that fortune cookie lucky numbers are selected by individuals who produce the numbers from their heads. If a mechanical process, random numbers table, or a computer algorithm that generates random numbers was the basis of the selection, the resulting lucky numbers would be uniformly distributed and the mean and minimum gap of a cookie's six lucky numbers would follow their theoretical distributions. The analysis also suggests that once the lucky numbers are selected, they are printed in multiples and inserted in a batch of cookies. As a result, cookies purchased from a particular location at a given point in time (as was the case with a majority of the cookies in the sonnet sample) produce an abnormally high number of matching sets of lucky numbers.

Reference

Boland, Philip J. and Yudi Pawitan (1999), "Trying to be Random in Selecting Numbers for Lotto," *Journal of Statistics Education*, Vol. 7, No. 3.

# ABOUT THE AUTHOR

Kim Bridgford is the director of the West Chester University Poetry Center and the West Chester University Poetry Conference. She is the author of three books of poetry: *Undone* (David Robert Books, 2003), nominated for the Pulitzer Prize; *Instead of Maps* (David Robert Books, 2005), nominated for the Poets' Prize; and *In the Extreme: Sonnets about World Records* (Story Line Press, 2007), winner of the Donald Justice Prize. With the visual artist Jo Yarrington, she is working on a three-book project, based on journey and sacred space, with photographs and sonnets on Iceland, Venezuela, and Bhutan. As the editor of *Mezzo Cammin,* she is the founder of The *Mezzo Cammin* Women Poets Timeline Project, which will eventually be the largest database of women poets in the world and was launched at the National Museum of Women in the Arts in Washington on March 27, 2010.

# ABOUT THE ARTIST

Jo Yarrington's drawings, photographs, and architecturally-based installations have been shown in exhibitions at the Aldrich Contemporary Art Museum, CT; Yale University, CT; Museum of Glass, WA; Contemporary Jewish Museum, San Francisco; DeCordova Museum and Sculpture Park, MA; Artists Space, NY; and William Benton Museum of Art, CT. International exhibitions have included Galeria Sala Uno, Italy; Centro de las Artes de Guanajuato, Mexico; Christuskirche, Germany; Glasgow School of Art, Scotland. She is a recipient of fellowships from the Pollock Krasner Foundation, the MacDowell Colony, SIMS/Iceland, the American Scandinavian Foundation, the Brandywine Institute, the Pennsylvania Council for the Arts, and the Connecticut Commission on Culture and Tourism. In 2001, she represented the United States at the Sharjah Biennial, United Arab Emirates. She is a Professor of Studio Art in the Department of Visual and Performing Arts at Fairfield University in Fairfield, CT. She lives and works in New York City and Norwalk, CT.

Made in the USA
Middletown, DE
18 September 2020

20113806R00050